Whose Chick is That?

JILL B. BRUCE

ILLUSTRATED BY JAN WADE

Kangaroo Press

Whose chick is that?

It's a black swan's chick!

Large black swans (*Cygnus atratus*) occur naturally only in Australia and are the bird emblem of Western Australia.

Black swans grow to 140 cm tall with a wingspan of up to 200 cm. They are black except for white-tipped wings and an orange-red **bill***. Females are slightly smaller than males and have a lighter-coloured bill. Like ducks, swans waterproof their feathers with oil from a gland just above their tail. During **preening** they stroke the oil onto their feathers with their beak.

These graceful birds live in most parts of Australia where there are large areas of water, either fresh, salt or **brackish**. They float high in the water and use their webbed feet to swim. In the air, large flocks fly in V-formation to find feeding grounds on swamps, pastures and mudflats. Swans are **herbivores**. They eat water plants and pasture grass near water.

While flying, they make a loud honking, trumpeting call. If they are threatened on land, they make an angry hissing sound. They gather on lakes and protected waters to **moult** their flight feathers between September and February each year. For the 2–3 weeks while moulting occurs, they cannot fly.

Swans have large, untidy nests of grass, leaves and sticks which they build near the water's edge. Most **clutches** have between 3–9 pale bluish-green eggs measuring

104 mm x 67 mm. Older birds mate for life but younger birds sometimes change mates. Both parents take turns **incubating** the eggs for 35–40 days and rearing the chicks. Even if threatened with death, the parents will not abandon their young. The downy, pale-grey cygnets swim and feed in the water soon after hatching.

Black swans are plentiful in wet areas of Australia and are fully **protected** by law.

* *See glossary on page 47.*

Whose chick is that?

It's a baby boobook owl!

Boobook owl chicks are naked when hatched. They remain helpless for several weeks.

Boobooks (*Ninox novaeseelandiae*) are the smallest Australian owl at 30–35 cm tall. These birds of prey have sharp talons and keen hearing. Their wings and back are dark brown and the breast is a light mottled beige but their colours can vary.

Boobooks are **nocturnal.** They **roost** by day in thick bush, caves or hollow trees and come out at dusk to hunt. Most people have heard the eerie 'mo-poke' or 'boo-book' call of these owls. Because of their call, they are also called mopokes.

Owls seem to have short necks, but they just have thick neck feathers. They can swivel their head right around and look down their own back. People say you can get them to twist their heads off by walking around them! Of course, this is not true.

Boobooks are found over most of Australia in many different **habitats** including deserts, forests and cities. They are the commonest and most widespread Australian owl. Insects make up most of their food but they also eat mice and small birds. Because they destroy insects and rodents these protected birds are useful to humans.

Boobook pairs select holes high up in tree trunks and the male prepares the nest of wood dust. The female lays 2–4 round, white eggs measuring 42 mm x 35 mm. She incubates them alone but the male brings her food while she is sitting on the eggs. After 33 days, the helpless young hatch. They learn to fly and leave the nest after six weeks.

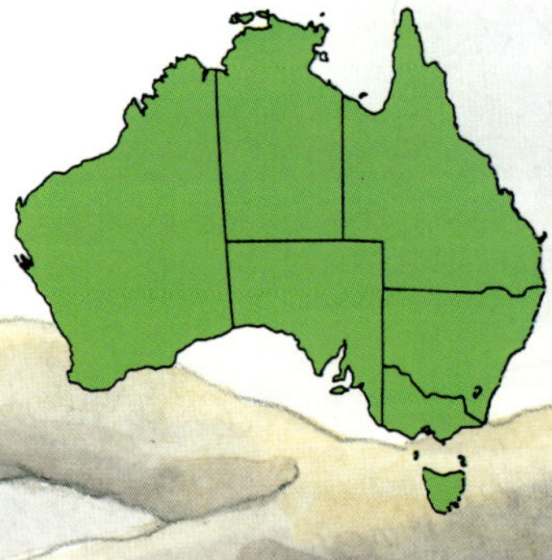

Whose chick is that?

This little grey ball of fluff is a brolga chick.

Brolgas (*Grus rubicundus*) are the only cranes native to Australia. They are the bird emblem of Queensland.

Brolgas are wading birds which stand over a metre tall on their long thin legs. They have light grey feathers, a long straight grey bill and yellow eyes. Their head colouring is very distinctive: a grey bald patch on top with red or orange around the head and neck.

Brolgas perform a spectacular 'dance'. A pair or sometimes large groups bow and stretch high and low. By flapping their wings they rise a metre off the ground and float gently back to earth like ballerinas. These birds are sacred to Aborigines and the dance of the brolgas is a traditional Aboriginal dance.

Brolgas are found in all states except Tasmania. They are very common in northern Australia but not found in large numbers in southern areas. Their favourite habitat is freshwater swamps containing bulkuru grass but they can also be found around grassy plains, farmlands, forest edges and saltwater lagoons. They can be heard making loud trumpeting calls and softer purring calls to their young and each other.

Brolgas are **omnivores**. They eat tubers of bulkuru grass, insects, shellfish, frogs and spiders plus maize and sorghum crops on farms.

Brolga pairs mate for life. They breed from September to March usually laying two 92 mm x 61 mm eggs that are off-white with small brown patches. The eggs may be laid on the bare ground or in large reedy nests at the waters edge. After 32 days the pale grey chicks hatch. The young fly after about 14 weeks but they stay with their parents until their third year. The parents then breed again. Brolgas are protected and quite plentiful but they are affected by habitat depletion and pollution.

Whose chick is that?

It's a budgerigar chick!

Budgerigar chicks are tiny, pink, helpless and naked when hatched but they soon grow downy feathers.

Budgerigars (*Melopsittacus undulatus*) are small parrots which grow up to 18 cm long. They are native to the Australian continent and have become a popular cage bird all over the world. They get their name from the Aboriginal word, *betcherrygah,* used on the Liverpool Plains in New South Wales.

In the wild budgerigars are yellow, green and brown but in captivity they have been bred to be white, blue, green and yellow. Both males and females are similar in **plumage** but on the male the patch of skin at the top of the bill, called a cere, is blue. In the female it is pale blue but it turns brown during breeding.

Huge flocks of budgerigars feed on grass seeds in the forest and grassland areas over much of inland Australia.The birds feed and drink in the early morning and rest during the heat of the day. They make a pleasing, chattering warble when content and a screech if alarmed. Budgerigars can be trained to **mimic** human speech.

Breeding seasons of budgerigars vary according to favourable rainfall. They nest in holes in trees, fence posts or fallen logs. The female lays 4–8 white rounded eggs measuring 19 mm x 14 mm. For the 18–20 days while she incubates the eggs, the male feeds her. Thirty days after hatching the chicks leave the nest and within a few days they can survive without any further parental care. Budgerigars will begin to breed when they are only three months old.

They are fully protected with no apparent decline in numbers since European settlement. Flocks of hundreds of thousands of budgerigars are still a common sight in some areas.

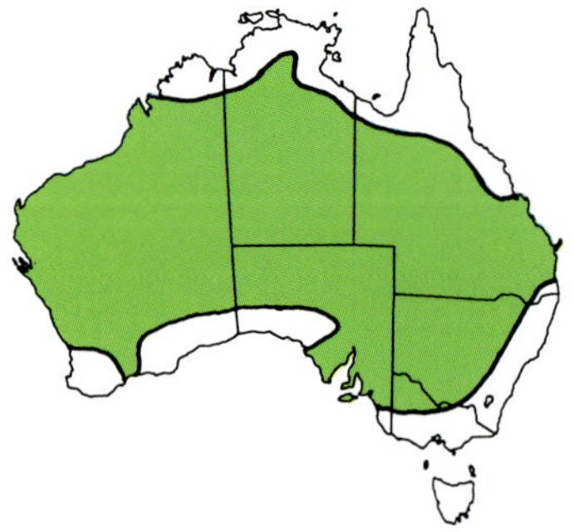

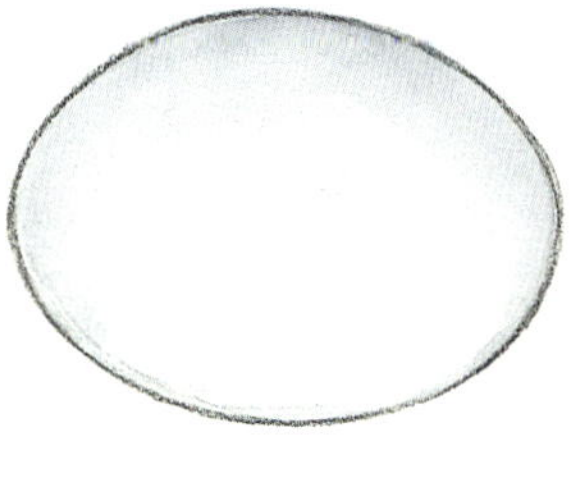

Whose chick is that?

This tiny chick is an eastern rosella.

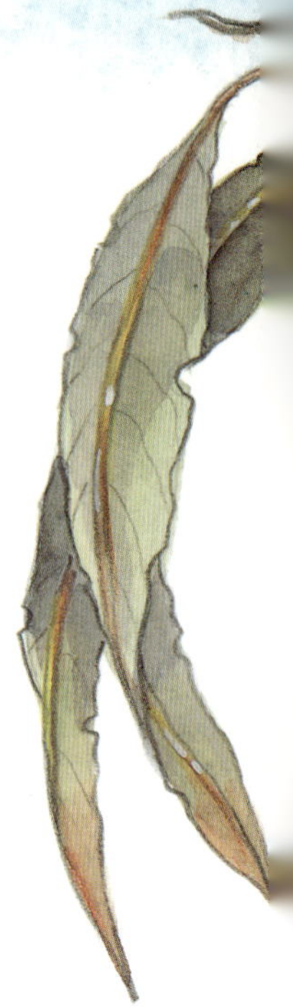

It is just beginning to grow its coloured feathers.

Eastern rosellas (*Platycercus eximius*) are very brightly coloured parrots about 30 centimetres long. They have a red head and chest, white cheeks, yellow belly and dark green lower abdomen and tail feathers. The wings are black, yellow and blue. The females are slightly smaller and their colours are a little duller than the males.

Eastern rosellas live in open forest country and partly cleared grasslands from south eastern Queensland to Victoria, South Australia and Tasmania. Their pleasant whistle sounds like 'clink-clink' when they are flying and 'pee pit-ee' while perched. They will feed in trees on wild fruits and berries but spend much of their time on the ground searching for grass seeds. Sometimes they raid and damage fruit orchards and other crops.

Rosellas breed in holes in trees, stumps and fence posts. In the breeding season between September to January the female lays 4–7 white eggs measuring 27 mm x 23 mm. The young are naked and helpless when hatched.

Because forests have been cleared for farming, their numbers have fallen, but they are still plentiful. They are totally protected.

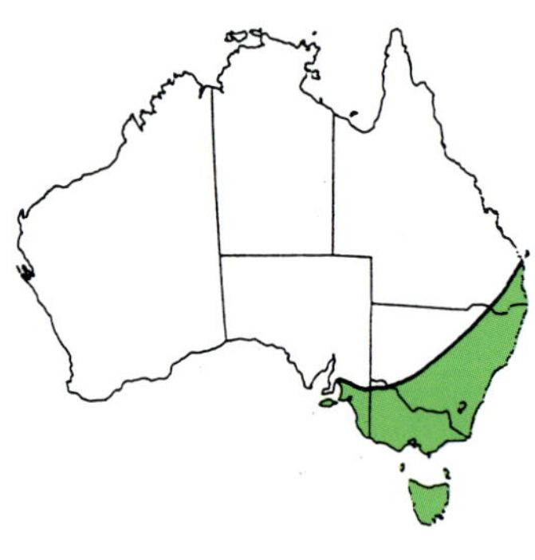

Whose chick is that?

This is an emu chick!

As soon as emu chicks hatch they are ready to follow their dad to find food.

The emu (*Dromaius novaehollandiae*) is the bird emblem of Australia and appears on the Australian coat of arms. Emus are the world's second largest bird. The biggest is the ostrich. Male emus grow up to 1.7 metres tall and weigh up to 50 kilograms. Females are slightly smaller except in the breeding season when they grow larger.

The neck of the male is usually a brighter blue than that of the female, but in the breeding season the female's neck also goes dark blue. The thick, grey-brown feathers of emus hide two small wings. They cannot fly although they run very fast on their long legs. Females make a deep drumming sound and the male utters belly grunts and low rumblings if excited or alarmed.

Emus live in lightly forested areas and grassy plains over a large area of mainland Australia avoiding deserts and closely settled areas. They feed on grass, seeds, fruit, flowers, caterpillars and grasshoppers. In some areas they break down fences and eat farm crops. To help them digest what they eat, they swallow stones to help grind food in their stomach.

The female emu lays up to ten large green eggs, weighing half a kilogram each and measuring 133 mm x 89 mm, in a grassy nest or on the sand. She then goes off and leaves the hatching and care of the young to the male. While incubating the eggs he loses five kilograms in weight. Male emus are very good parents who protect the striped chicks for about eight months. The stripes fade as the chicks grow and their plumage turns grey-brown.

Emus are plentiful across the continent with no danger of extinction but they are protected.

Whose chick is that?

It's a kookaburra chick!

This kookaburra chick has a beak as thick as its parents' beak but not as long.

Kookaburras (*Dacelo novaeguineae*) at 46 cm long are the largest kingfisher in the world. They are the state bird of New South Wales. Their name comes from an Aboriginal word for the sound they make. The loud laughing cry of the kookaburra is one of Australia's best-known bird calls. They are at their noisiest at sunrise and sunset and their chuckles are thought to indicate ownership of territory. Because of their call, they are also known as the laughing jackass.

Kookaburras have a creamy-white, squat body with brown wings and brown feathers on top of the head and behind the eyes. Sometimes males have bright blue and females light blue feathers on their wings. Their very large, strong beaks are used to catch and kill prey. They hold small snakes in their beak while they beat them to death on a tree. Kookaburras live up to 25 years and consume insects, lizards, snakes, worms, mice, crabs, fish, and small birds.

Originally found only in open forests and woodlands of eastern Australia, they have been introduced to Tasmania and Western Australia. They are not popular in these states because they attack small native birds.

Kookaburras mate for life. They lay two or three white eggs, measuring 46 x 36 mm, in a hole in a tree, in a termite nest or an earth bank. The naked chicks hatch after 25–28 days. Unpaired birds in their small family group often help the pair incubate and feed their hungry chicks. These fully protected birds are quite common.

Whose chick is that?

It's a lyrebird chick!

When hatched, lyrebird chicks do not have long tail feathers. These grow later.

The superb lyrebird (*Menura novaehollandiae*) which is shown on Australia's ten-cent coin, is so named because of the male's incredible tail feathers. These are shaped like an ancient musical instrument, the lyre. The males are dark grey-brown birds, 90–95 cm long, including their silver grey, brown and white tail. The female is smaller and has an attractive brown fantail.

Lyrebirds do not fly very well and so to roost in trees at night they use short flapping jumps. They are found in rugged, forested country on the east coast of Australia from Stanthorpe in Queensland down to Melbourne in Victoria and have been introduced to Tasmania.

Lyrebirds are **diurnal** and spend all day scratching with their large feet and long claws through leaves and debris searching for insects, worms and snails.

When the male lyrebird is looking for mates, he builds up to twelve dancing mounds. Here he sings his own songs and mimics all sorts of other sounds. When a female appears he spreads his superb tail feathers over his head like an open fan, sings and dances backward and forward to attract her.

Males take no part in looking after eggs or chicks. In the winter breeding season, females build large bulky nests on rock ledges, on the top of tall stumps or at the base of trees. They make their side-opening nest of twigs, sticks, mosses and dry fern leaves. The inside is lined with roots and bark fibre and downy feathers.

Female lyrebirds lay one egg which can vary from light grey to deep purplish-brown with streaks and spots. The 65 mm x 45 mm egg hatches after 42 days. The young bird stays in the nest for six weeks and may be fed by the female for up to a year.

Lyrebirds mimic at least twenty other calls and sounds, especially of other birds in their area. They have several calls of their own, the most common being a 'choo-choo-choo' sound. These shy, totally protected birds live deep in quiet forests and their survival is threatened by forest destruction.

Whose chick is that?

It's a baby magpie!

Don't even think of touching it or getting too close or you may be dive-bombed by an angry adult magpie.

Magpies are large black and white birds which grow up to 40 centimetres long. There are two colour forms of the Australian magpie. The black-backed magpie (*Gymnorhina tibicen*) found over most of mainland Australia, is the bird emblem of South Australia. The white-backed magpie is found in South Australia, Victoria, southern New South Wales and Tasmania. The western magpie, found in the south of Western Australia is also white-backed. Scientists see them all as one **species** because they interbreed where their territories overlap.

Magpies live in open woodlands, pastures and suburban areas with trees, feeding on insects, **carrion**, and small reptiles. Their pleasant, melodious carolling call is often sung in chorus by a group of birds.

Magpies live in groups, from two to twenty birds, with a dominant male who mates with more than one female. They build deep, bowl-shaped nests of twigs and sticks and line them with grass and fur. To be safe from **predators** the nests are at least ten metres up in tall trees. The 2–6 eggs, measuring 38 x 27 mm, are pale-green streaked with reddish-brown. Females build the nest and incubate the eggs alone but the group helps feed and care for the chicks. Incubation takes twenty days and the helpless chicks stay in the nest for four weeks.

Magpies are protected, widespread and common. They seem, if anything, to have increased in numbers with European settlement.

Whose chick is that?

It's a baby sulphur-crested cockatoo!

Cute, but sort of ugly, is one way to describe the baby sulphur-crested cockatoo. Sulphur-crested cockatoos are one of Australia's best-known and most numerous cockatoos. When kept as cage pets they can be taught to 'talk' or mimic sounds and do tricks.

The white sulphur-crested cockatoo (*Cacatua galerita*) stands up to 50 cm tall. When alarmed, it raises its yellow crest feathers and shrieks raucously. Male and female birds are the same size and colour but they can be identified by their eyes: males have black eyes and the females' eyes are ruby red.

Cockatoos are protected and plentiful as they have adjusted well to living next to humans. They are found in a wide range of habitats from wooded urban areas, to rainforests, mangrove swamps and woodlands along northern and eastern mainland Australia, Tasmania and around a small section of coastal Western Australia.

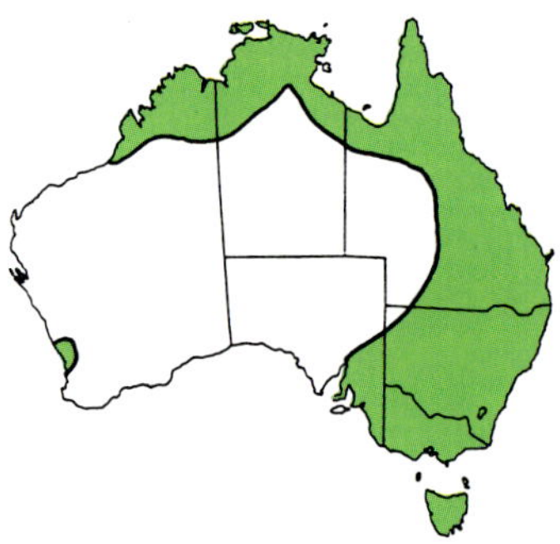

They eat seeds, plants, roots, berries and insects. Sometimes they raid and damage crops. When feeding on the ground, cockatoos leave one bird on guard. If danger threatens, its loud cry warns the others to fly away.

Two to three white eggs measuring 47 mm x 34 mm are laid in nesting holes in trees and cliffs. Both parents share the 28–day incubation of the eggs. The naked and dependent chicks remain in the nest until they have grown their feathers at six weeks. They have been known to live up to fifty years.

Whose chick is that?

These chicks are wedge-tailed eagles!

You can tell by the curved beak that these downy, helpless chicks are wedge-tailed eagles.

This majestic bird of prey (*Aquila audax*) is found throughout most of Australia in deserts, forested areas, mountains and islands, and it is the bird emblem of the Northern Territory.

Male wedge-tailed eagles stand about a metre tall with a wing span of over two metres. The females are slightly smaller. They are the world's fourth largest eagle.

Like all **raptors**, they have hooked beaks and sharp talons. Wedge-tailed eagles are superb fliers who swoop down from great heights to catch prey. These diurnal hunters eat rabbits, dingoes, kangaroos, birds, lambs and **carrion**.

Wedge-tailed eagles have tawny brown to black feathers and a wedge-shaped tail. Their legs are covered with feathers right down to the feet. They have a piercing screech and they also make quiet yelps and squeals.

Wedge-tailed eagles mate for life. They build huge nests of sticks and branches which they line with fresh gum leaves. Usually the nests are high in trees or cliffs so they have a good view of the surrounding area. One or two white or cream eggs with dull red blotches are laid about June or July. Both parents help incubate the 73 mm x 58 mm eggs and look after the eaglets. The chicks do not fly until they are three months old and often only one chick survives. Wedge-tailed eagles numbers are secure as they are protected by law but farmers still shoot them in some areas. Because they eat animals and birds which are part of a larger food chain, they are often found to have high levels of insecticide in their bodies. This kills the birds and causes their eggs to be infertile.

Australian birds and their young

Australia has some of the world's most beautiful and unusual birds. Over 700 native species and many introduced birds are found in Australia. Like every other animal the young resemble their parents, but do not resemble them totally until they are fully grown.

Depending on the type of bird, hatched chicks can be helpless and totally naked with their eyes closed, or covered in fluffy down, or fully feathered and ready to run about and feed. Ground and water-nesting birds are usually feathered and can run when they hatch but tree-nesting birds are mostly naked and helpless. This means emu and swan chicks have feathers and are ready to move and feed as soon as they are hatched but parrot and kookaburra chicks are naked and dependent when hatched. They need to be kept warm, protected and fed by the parents for up to three months.

The egg colours given in this book are for newly laid eggs. Egg colour varies, even in the same species. Many eggs change colour within the incubation time and eggs may get dirty in the nest.

Nearly half of all eggs laid and young hatchlings are destroyed by predators. Snakes, goannas, other bird species, rats and mice, possums and sometimes humans are the enemies. The sun, wind and rain also destroy eggs and kill young birds.

It is very important not to disturb birds at their nests. If you see a nest, do not touch it as many birds will abandon nests that have been interfered with. Do not stay near nests for long as parent birds get very anxious about their young. If left unattended for too long eggs may get cold and the young could die before hatching. Use binoculars rather than moving too close to nests. Do not for any reason collect eggs or nests as there are laws in every state of Australia against egg or nest collection.

Some bird species are losing the fight to breed and survive because their habitat is being destroyed or changed, or they are affected by pollution. Many are killed by feral predators like cats, rats and foxes.

Many species of Australian birds will come into your garden to feed if you grow flowering native plants like bottlebrush or grevillea. A birdbath filled with water will also attract colourful, singing wildlife. Birds, as well as being beautiful, eat insects and snails and pollinate the flowers. If we all care for our native birds they will be there for our children's children.

Glossary

BILL	The beak of a bird
BRACKISH	A mixture of salt and fresh water
CARNIVORE	An animal that eats other animals
CARRION	The rotting flesh of dead animals
CLUTCH	A group of eggs in a bird's nest
DIURNAL	Active in the daytime
HABITAT	The environment where an animal naturally lives in the wild
HERBIVORE	An animal that eats only plants
INCUBATE	Hatching eggs by sitting on them to keep them warm
MIMIC	To repeat sounds and words without understanding them
MOULT	To shed the feathers or skin before new ones grow
NOCTURNAL	Active in the night-time
OMNIVORE	An animal that eats plants and animals
PLUMAGE	All the feathers on a bird
PREDATOR	An animal that catches and kills other animals for food
PREEN	To oil and tidy the feathers with the beak
PROTECTED	Animals or plants that laws try to save from destruction
RAPTOR	A bird of prey like hawks and eagles
ROOST	A place where birds settle and stay for the night
SPECIES	A scientific grouping of animals that are the same

Index

For Milton Peter, our little chickadee, with love.
J.B.B

Acknowledgments

The author and illustrator appreciate the helpful information given by Jim Benham, 'The bird man of Bayview'.

First published in 1995 by Kangaroo Press Pty Ltd
3 Whitehall Road Kenthurst NSW 2156 Australia
PO Box 6125 Dural Delivery Centre NSW 2158
Printed in Hong Kong through Colorcraft Ltd

ISBN 0 86417 576 0